The LEAVES

RON LOEWINSOHN

Black Sparrow Press / Los Angeles / 1973

LIBRARY OF CONGRESS CATALOGING IN PUBLICATION DATA

Loewinsohn, Ron
   The leaves.

   Poems.
   I. Title.
PS3523.032L4   811'.5'4   73-1309
ISBN 0-87685-147-2
ISBN 0-87685-146-4 (pbk.)

BLACK SPARROW PRESS
P. O. Box 25603
Los Angeles, Ca. 90025

this one is for
the lady in the tree

THE LEAVES

THE LEAVES [1]

There had been a body
          white
among the branches
          warm &
close I moved toward you
          supple
limbs, hair, breasts swollen
          then
filled because no emptiness
          could
be; I believed in you in
          your presence
I was leaved, full of us, there
          was no
silence, no bare moment, no
          ending
but each day resonant with
          the day
before. Now the days are
          filled
with sunlight, the appletrees are
          white
charged fields of smells, bee-sounds &
          apple-growth
& having seen them again
          I want
that tension, filled up with
          wanting
it, what's left, & how now to move
          toward it

THE LEAVES [2]

The moon again painfully bright
  moving among the clouds.
Above the apple trees the clouds
  themselves like limbs burdened
with petals in early April. The cold
  dark air between them is gone
& the moon as it enters bodies them
  with light for a moment & leaves
them. There are more. All night long
  after I left the porch to go back
into the house the moon moved
  among the clouds. Like the sleeves
of a loose gown they fell back
  from her brightness even tho
the bare arms inside them reached
  upward in longing toward her.
All night long above the roofs, above
  the trees the moon leaving
one night last week it goes on leaving
  the clouds.

THE LEAVES [3]

There was a brightness in the branches
that was a body, a white clarity
I saw in there among a cloud of
apple blossoms & green leaves. Her arms
were a little chubby & her legs dangled
down; she smiled at me a dark-eyed
smile, & her nipples as she sat
on her branch, & the line her legs made
where they met her body, & her dark
pubic hair, made another smile, a rich,
heavy body, filled with her own presence &
with the greenness of the leaves, but so white,
& leaving, wherever she smiled, a flowering
longing for that clear, heavy fullness.

THE LEAVES [4]

And once she became herself
a tree, a radiant whiteness
of body within her
gauzy, cloudlike blouse between
the moon & me. Or
she was herself the moon
bodying with light her own
cloud, her own leaves.

THE LEAVES [5]

One morning you woke up & the trees
just beyond the open window spilled
their freshness into the room, blue &
early, the air moving gently thru the
leaves. The branches were full of
darknesses which also moved as the limbs
stretched up & over the roofs. Later
the day would be hot, but now the woman
beside you had thrown back the one
sheet that had covered you both.
Her shoulder where you kissed it was
cool and the smile that came to her face then
was private, a smile for herself alone
tho there was left for you the pleasure of
watching it, watching her dark hair,
the dark hollow the bend of her arm
made where her hand went under
her cheek. Deep within herself a belief
in you had flowered, & this is what she
smiled at then, a dark, private, silent
pleasure, fragile as a leaf. She knew
you would leave her & you left her.

THE LEAVES [6]

It was
here
now

THE LEAVES [7]

The whole sequence is a maze-
    like dance that defines
the space it takes up by using it,
    by taking it up.
The dance floor is the floor where the dance occurs,
    defined by the use of it.
It's left
    as before, except that now
it's entered
    into the gesture by which the dancer
asserts the relation of herself
    as qualified by it, among
other things.
            I can imagine her threading
    her way thru the rows of multi-
colored corn, weaving the field anew
    as a potent thanksgiving.
But here, walking under the bare
    branches of the trees, it's the sky
that's made over within
    the branches, within
the field they define, a little
    darker, & made up
of—even more than the painful
    angles & traceries of the smaller
branches—of the spaces they suggest,
    constantly & subtly changing as the
afternoon breeze moves casually thru them
    dancing itself.

She decided then to leave
        the ground & take
up some of that space, sitting
        on one of the larger
limbs with her legs dangling,
        the blue canvas
shoes still on her feet
        which she allowed to sway slightly.
She had thought first to leave
        her clothes on the ground, but
now carried them in a compact
        bundle under her arm, having
taken them off when she decided
        to move up into the world
of brown branches & black twigs,
        tho now these aren't bare but
redolent of broad
        flat leaves each as big
as a hand, a dark dusty
        green on top & a paler
green on the underside which was also
        complexly veined.
She couldn't explain why she'd ascended;
        she could never have predicted it,
nor that the bark of the branch she
        sat on would be deeply textured &
imprint itself temporarily (& with a
        slightly pleasant pain) on her buttocks,
nor that she would find fine
        white scratches along her shins &

(*16*)

the tender underside of her forearms
    where she'd scraped them in
climbing, nor that weeks later she
    would notice the skin of her
arms & miss those scratches, which had
    faded along with the tan she'd
gotten that summer. Now
    she sat in a dark volume of
flat leaves, a white radiance moving
    a little clumsily above me, smiling
deeply unto herself, but without
    the grace I expect from tree creatures.

THE LEAVES [8]

O radiant, pudgy lady
of delicate, long lashes &
plump limbs, O branch
made warm by the cheeks
of her ass, O tree to which
the branch is attached, or
tree realized in branching,
made actual in a poem of
dark, flat leaves amid whose
darknesses the moon seemed
to move, O dense occurance of
dark vowels & a white hand
reaching up to the branch above
your head & bending down
with your weight the branch you
sit on—leave me now,
in your absence realized in
reaching, becoming in a
dark fluttering of words,
a constant discovering movement
in a dense volume moving

THE LEAVES [9]

What is it that I want
         to say to you? your pale eyes
have depths I want to enter
         pale green. Reaching up into
the tree, a green space or shade
         the light comes thru the leaves
like that, a depth of leaves.
         Reaching up to them, or into them
out of an aching blackness inside me
         leaves the blackness inside me.

                         You gave me a ring
                         of gold, with a black stone
                         an old ring that belonged
                         to a silly old woman now
                         rotting in her grave. Grape leaves
                         of gold surround that black stone.

Wrap your arms & legs around me, finest
         down on your limbs lit by the lamp
beside our bed as my mouth finds yours.
         Palest green and gold light I'll
always be reaching to enter
         those depths which is me leaving me,
leaved in reaching to find me in
         the space we create, the tree
we make that leaves us each together.

THE ACE OF CUPS

All day long & all night
the cup is offered, the rain
raining down, or a well of water
springing up out of the chalice
& descending in a shower of tongues
of flame, tongues of flame mirrored
by the burning flowers of the pond
which turn their mouths up to the cloud
above them & the hand there reaching
to offer the cup each moment.
The Host also is a daily offering:
the dove who holds it in his bill
holds it forever above the water
as it spills clear as a single word
spoken once all day long & all night
raining down & waiting only
to be taken. Take it.

THE LEAVES [10]   *for Mike Davidson*

What is it but a self-
assertion, a prideful
climbing

                There is a voice for a poet,
                a spilling

simultaneously a denial
of pride, a return to a kind
of childhood

                      not of words but
                of a single word that re-
                sounds in all words

with all its scraped shins &
palms from the bark they
move among

                I heard it again Thursday
                from Mike. It's a tall word
                with an animal darkness & heavi-
                ness at its center, a small
                word filled with music & light,
                a rasping, furry quickness
                & a spikey, leafy brightness
                on top, a clear tone, clear &
                hard as a jewel in a ring, thru
                which we see the light that fills
                the stone, bringing it into full
                being

You learned the weight of your own
body, of your own head even,
when your arms & fingers reached
for the branch to pull yourself, to
lift your own weight, feeling
your fingers straining
at the rough wood & the push
in your feet pressing against
the trunk, hefting yourself, lunging
forward with your head,
& quickly grabbing
at the next branch,
up into that green &
apple-smelling dimness the leaves made.

                    It occurs in the air
                as the air itself does, there
                whether we hear it or not.

To climb like that—to pull & smell
your own salty skin & the heavy,
earthy smell of the bark, to know
your own heavy breathing & the moving
glints of light that pierces
the leaves—to climb like that
is to dance with the tree,
to enter into that dance of ground & moving
air, of woody matter & light &
fingers reaching out of the self & chlorophyl
& weight & flat fleshy leaves
each the size of a hand.

(*22*)

The voice is a familiar
relation, an old story
in which we find ourselves
anew, & the orders
in which we occur & will

Wasn't it to find yourself again
that you climbed up into the tree
to begin with that dark green filled with
pre-dawn freshness for once & so
peeled off what you called your
city-skin, those clothes

As such the voice is a presence
that seizes the chest & throat
from within, welling up & spill-
ing in a laugh that throws the head
back & the whole trunk of the
body collapses against the back
of the chair

that had defined you & now
you felt the first stirrings of the air
as it moved the fine hair on your
arms & your pubis, a thrill
of awakened skin & lungs filled
with air whose freshness is felt
at the back of the throat

                              or a cry that curls your
                    fingers in your hair as the heels of
                    your hands come up to your temples
                    & looking down thru your tears
                    you see only your own breasts caught
                    & pressed between the sockets of
                    your elbows, locked & trembling as
                    the voice is now you spilling
                    over so heavy your knees give
                    way & you sink to the ground,

as you reach up, lunging into
that space the leaves make, a light
like a morning in summer just
before the sun rises—cool & blue-green,
sharp with the smell of sap & leaf. & now
your own weight, your own actions & movements have
set the tree—No. The tree responds
to your weight & actions by entering itself
into the dance, coming itself
into the actual & even the vocal,
declaring itself in sound & gesture,
a dark volume of moving light
& growth & limbs reaching, a
flowering choir where now you are

                    or a single syllable you
                    speak always with your arms
                    around her & your face
                    in her hair.

                         (24)

The choir is the place where the choir
sings or dances, or sings & dances,
the moving limbs you embrace, you walk
on & lean on, breathing in time to your own
breathing, a hedge-like enclosure, a space
related to a garden, a made place grasped
by the hand from what surrounds it—
not only grasped but entered into, not only
danced in but danced with, the breathing
itself a dancing of lights within the dimness
the tree makes.

    The voice is a feeling
    in the throat, vibrations
    of flesh, cords—the thread
    or path of the story related to
    us originating in the darkness
    of the chest (lungs) & throat—
    flowering out into the air it's
    made of
       —like the voice that spoke to me
    in the dream, explaining that the young woman
    running or skipping down the road bordered
    by trees & hedges ran or skipped simply
    from excess of, from sheer—she was in
    love & love made her run so
    that as she passed each tree I saw it
    flame out into glowing life in a narrow band
    where she passed it, a blossoming zone
    on the tree which everywhere else stayed

summer-green, dark & containing
its own life. The bushes she ran past
likewise flowered where her feet had drawn
near. But as I followed I saw the leaves
up close: their gold was an autumn gold,
a red & yellow of November.
& when I'd overtaken her she reached up
her hand, swinging playfully at an over-
hanging bough, changing the leaves to brilliant
white flowers, snowdrops. Yet when I
reached up my own hand to touch them they were
snowflakes, & then the day was blotted out
instantly in a blinding squall of snow as
the voice made clear

    But to turn or re-
turn to that garden is also to leave
the ground, to become for me
a whiteness within the moving
branches I reach toward as the branches
reach themselves toward the moon.
An indulgence time won't abide. When
Willie climbed up into the tree
he became another instance of that
white presence among the dark leaves,
his weight animating the branches.
He was then both a celebration of the
possible & an instance of its loss.
& I too, looking up at him from the ground I
stood on, had become both

himself basking in my concern &
myself at his age looking down
at the bare ground beneath the tree.
I can't leave it alone.

     It was, too, the voice
     that came out of my own throat
     as I awoke from that dream—
     a cross between a bark & a
     groan as death came clear & I
     reached over toward you
     —a voice that comes
     from one darkness into another,
     a cry that creates that dark room
     as it returns to my ear, bringing
     a sense of the true darkness in those
     snowflakes that were blooming branches,
     death like a seed germinating, emerging

The dance then is a declaration
an articulation of yourself in all
your branchings & turnings, yourself
a tree bodied with light coming
into the eye or out of the eye,
your head bowed slightly down
a whiteness within the further dark
of your hair, yet moving as the tree
allows, the body swayed
to a music you hear as

     the voice which occurs all the time
     while everything else is happening.

(27)

169

*Printed February 1973 in Santa Barbara for the
Black Sparrow Press by Noel Young. Design by
Barbara Martin. This edition is limited
to 1000 copies in paper wrappers; there are
200 copies numbered and signed by the poet;
and 26 copies handbound in boards by Earle Gray,
lettered and signed by the poet.*

Ron Loewinsohn was born in the Philippines
in 1937 & has lived in the United States since
1945, mostly in the San Francisco Bay Area.
He now lives in Berkeley, where he teaches at
the University of California (American Lit.).
The Leaves is part of a new collection of
poems he's now working on, called *Goat Dances*.
He is also working on a study of W. C. Williams'
early development.